AF266708

DINOSAUR SEASONS

by

SUSAN LAMANNA VERZULLI

Illustrated by
Emmanuel Dinardi

Graphic Design by
Michael Park

Dedicated to my awesome granddaughters

PURPLE OWL PUBLISHING

Newton, MA 02461

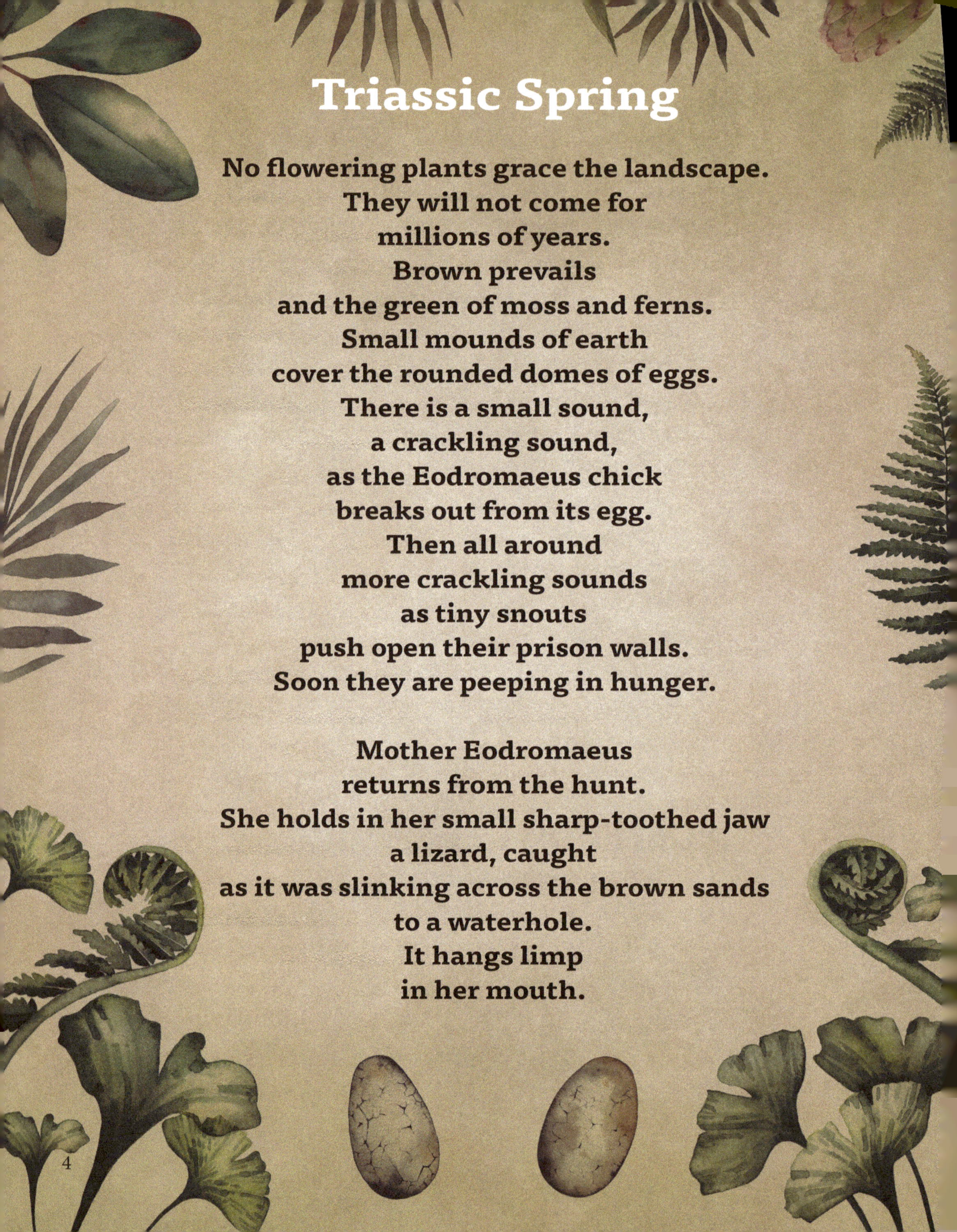

Triassic Spring

No flowering plants grace the landscape.
They will not come for
millions of years.
Brown prevails
and the green of moss and ferns.
Small mounds of earth
cover the rounded domes of eggs.
There is a small sound,
a crackling sound,
as the Eodromaeus chick
breaks out from its egg.
Then all around
more crackling sounds
as tiny snouts
push open their prison walls.
Soon they are peeping in hunger.

Mother Eodromaeus
returns from the hunt.
She holds in her small sharp-toothed jaw
a lizard, caught
as it was slinking across the brown sands
to a waterhole.
It hangs limp
in her mouth.

The babies peep loudly
as mother Eodromaeus
bites off a piece of her prize
to feed them.
Spring passes.
Out of twelve babies
four are left.
Always hungry, now learning
to hunt on their own
as this Triassic spring
becomes summer.

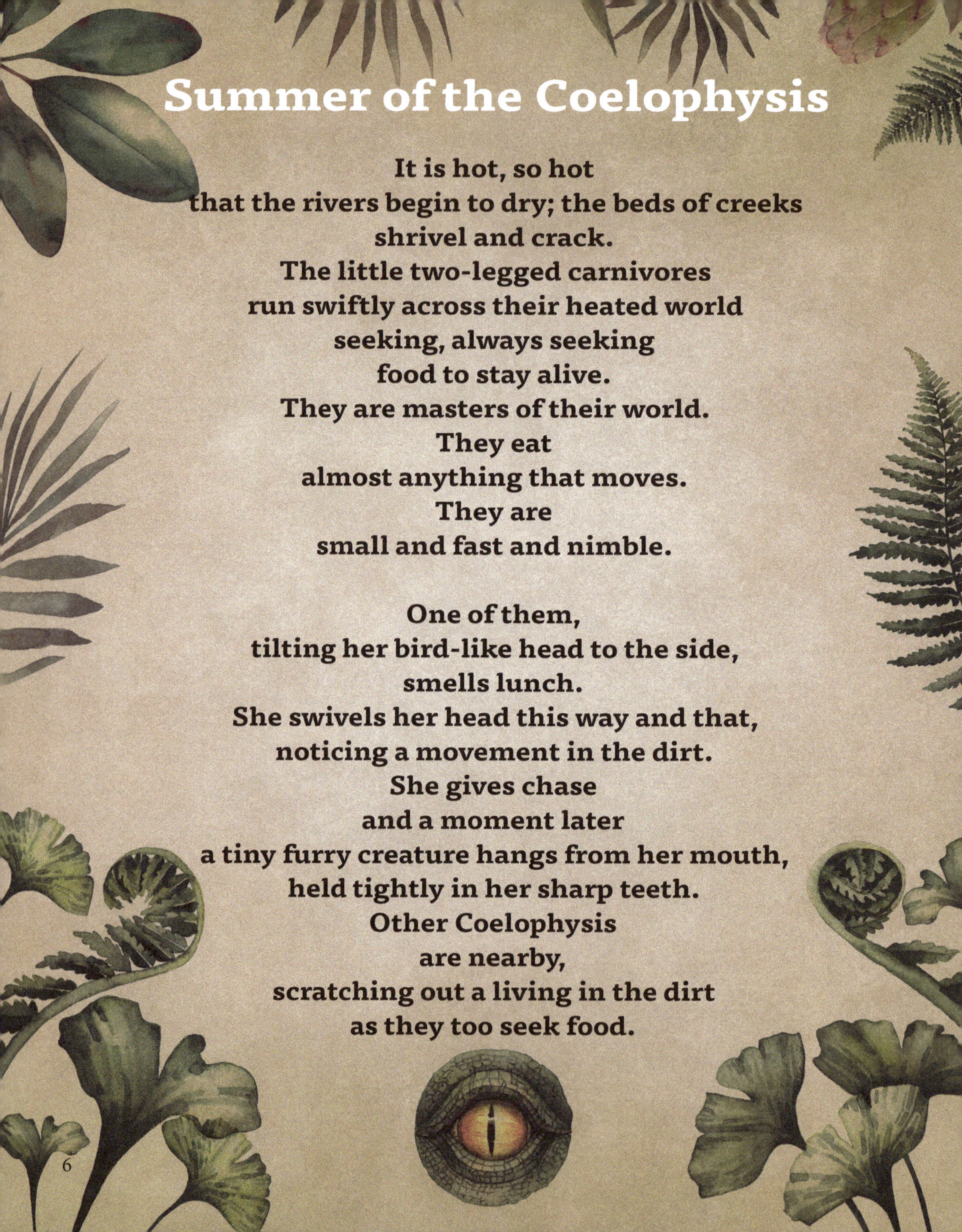

Summer of the Coelophysis

It is hot, so hot
that the rivers begin to dry; the beds of creeks
shrivel and crack.
The little two-legged carnivores
run swiftly across their heated world
seeking, always seeking
food to stay alive.
They are masters of their world.
They eat
almost anything that moves.
They are
small and fast and nimble.

One of them,
tilting her bird-like head to the side,
smells lunch.
She swivels her head this way and that,
noticing a movement in the dirt.
She gives chase
and a moment later
a tiny furry creature hangs from her mouth,
held tightly in her sharp teeth.
Other Coelophysis
are nearby,
scratching out a living in the dirt
as they too seek food.

**Food is not abundant
in the dry season but it will come again
with the rains.**

Rainy Season

Furry things in this distant time
are small, as small as rats,
still not fully mammal.
They lay their eggs
and care for their young.
The reptiles rule this world.
The dinosaurs
this early in Dinosaur Time, the Triassic,
are not yet dominant
but are on their way to becoming
the rulers of the land.
Now the rains are coming.

They start slowly,
then a cloudburst.
The proto mammals called Cynodonts
nestle deep into their burrows.
The dinosaurs,
Plateosaurus and her kin,
browse for plants in the raindrops,
drink from puddles.
They will thrive
and their kind will rule the Earth
for many seasons to come.

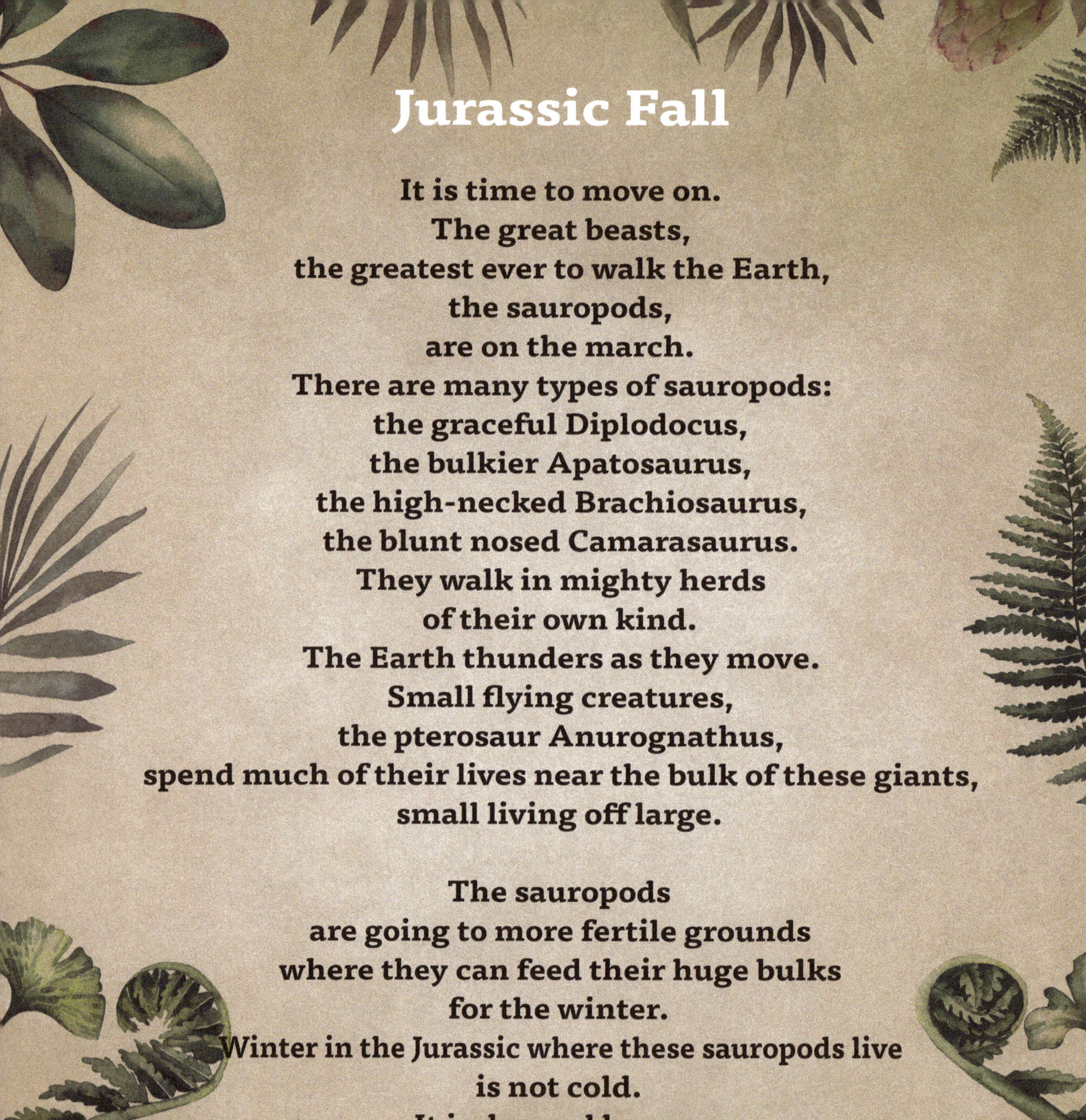

Jurassic Fall

It is time to move on.
The great beasts,
the greatest ever to walk the Earth,
the sauropods,
are on the march.
There are many types of sauropods:
the graceful Diplodocus,
the bulkier Apatosaurus,
the high-necked Brachiosaurus,
the blunt nosed Camarasaurus.
They walk in mighty herds
of their own kind.
The Earth thunders as they move.
Small flying creatures,
the pterosaur Anurognathus,
spend much of their lives near the bulk of these giants,
small living off large.

The sauropods
are going to more fertile grounds
where they can feed their huge bulks
for the winter.
Winter in the Jurassic where these sauropods live
is not cold.
It is dry and barren
but these giants will always find food.

Their long necks
reach into the highest branches.
They walk in great herds,
the younger ones between the elders for protection.
They browse for food as they go.
They must eat almost constantly
to fuel their great bodies.
Their robust necks and horse-like heads
reach for the leaves and fronds
higher up than any other living creature has reached
before or since.

Pliosaur Afternoon

Sunlight filters down
into the ocean depths
until it gets so deep
it is too dark to see.
The monster
glides huge flippers,
each one longer than a human,
through the green waters
of the late Jurassic.
Rising toward the surface
of the water,
he must breathe,
for he is not a fish.
He is a reptile,
a giant sea monster.
He is not a dinosaur,
for no dinosaur was fully aquatic,
but a distant cousin.

As he glides toward the sunlight
of the day above
he spots a fishlike shape,
an ichthyosaur,
swimming swiftly away
but not swiftly enough
for the giant jaws of Pliosaurus.

In one bite
it is all over.
Full now,
Pliosaurus
continues to swim upward
toward the air,
toward the sun.

Time of the Chase

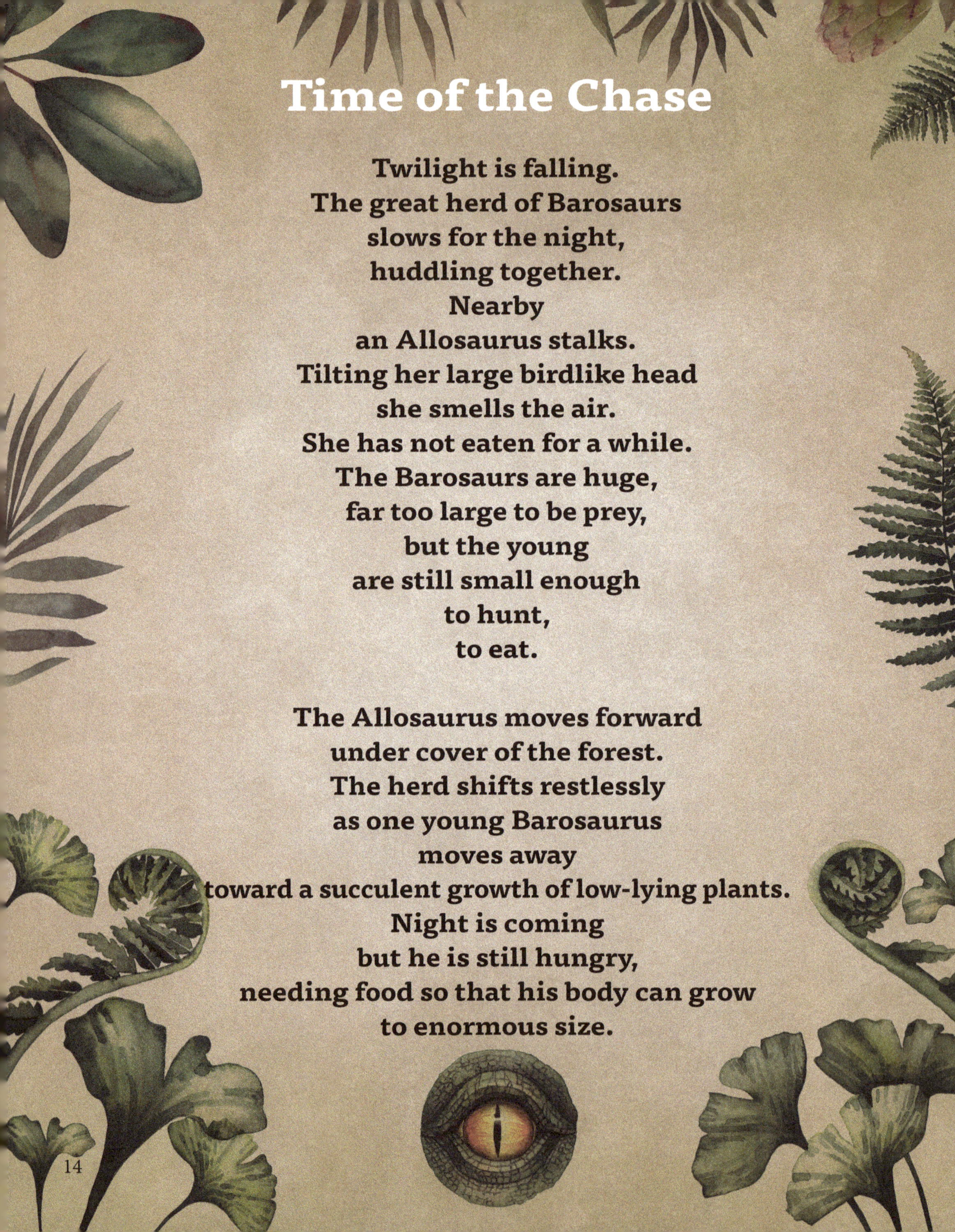

Twilight is falling.
The great herd of Barosaurs
slows for the night,
huddling together.
Nearby
an Allosaurus stalks.
Tilting her large birdlike head
she smells the air.
She has not eaten for a while.
The Barosaurs are huge,
far too large to be prey,
but the young
are still small enough
to hunt,
to eat.

The Allosaurus moves forward
under cover of the forest.
The herd shifts restlessly
as one young Barosaurus
moves away
toward a succulent growth of low-lying plants.
Night is coming
but he is still hungry,
needing food so that his body can grow
to enormous size.

The Allosaurus smells
him nearby
and leaps forward, all
slashing teeth.
Alarmed,
the young one
turns back toward the
herd.
The Allosaurus gives
chase.
She is almost upon him,
reaching her head,
opening her great jaws,
teeth gleaming sharp.

Suddenly
a gigantic Barosaurus appears,
rearing up toward the
Allosaurus
and swinging her mighty neck.
The young one
scurries to safety.
The Allosaurus stops,
her slow brain startled,
then she turns away.
Dinner
will have to wait.

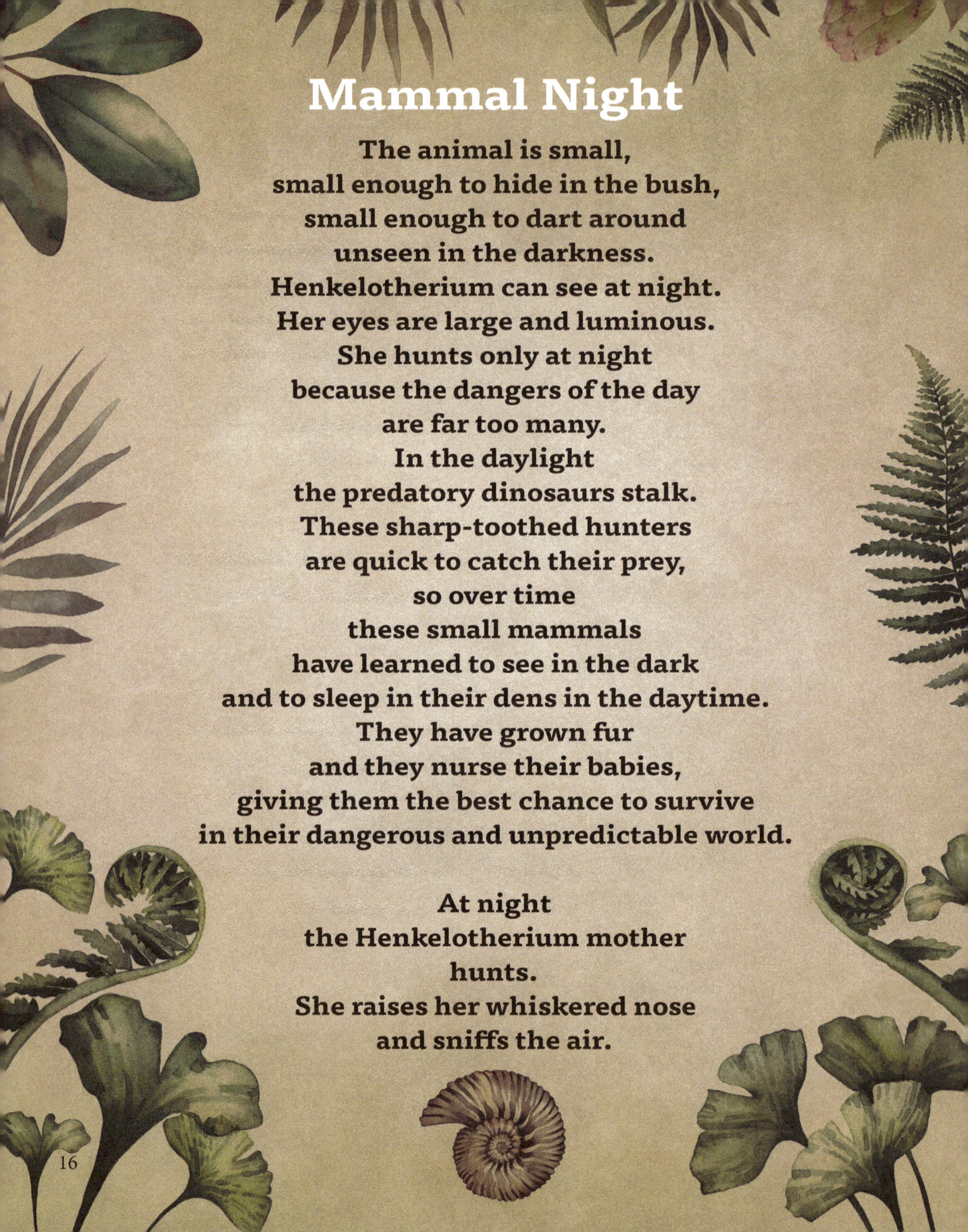

Mammal Night

The animal is small,
small enough to hide in the bush,
small enough to dart around
unseen in the darkness.
Henkelotherium can see at night.
Her eyes are large and luminous.
She hunts only at night
because the dangers of the day
are far too many.
In the daylight
the predatory dinosaurs stalk.
These sharp-toothed hunters
are quick to catch their prey,
so over time
these small mammals
have learned to see in the dark
and to sleep in their dens in the daytime.
They have grown fur
and they nurse their babies,
giving them the best chance to survive
in their dangerous and unpredictable world.

At night
the Henkelotherium mother
hunts.
She raises her whiskered nose
and sniffs the air.

She smells a tiny lizard nearby,
resting under the ferns.
Moving forward slowly
then jumping suddenly,
Henkelotherium finds herself
with a mouthful of tiny scales.
The lizard had no chance.
Soon after
she finds another.
Full and satisfied,
she returns to her den as the
sun comes up
to feed her babies
and to sleep away the day.

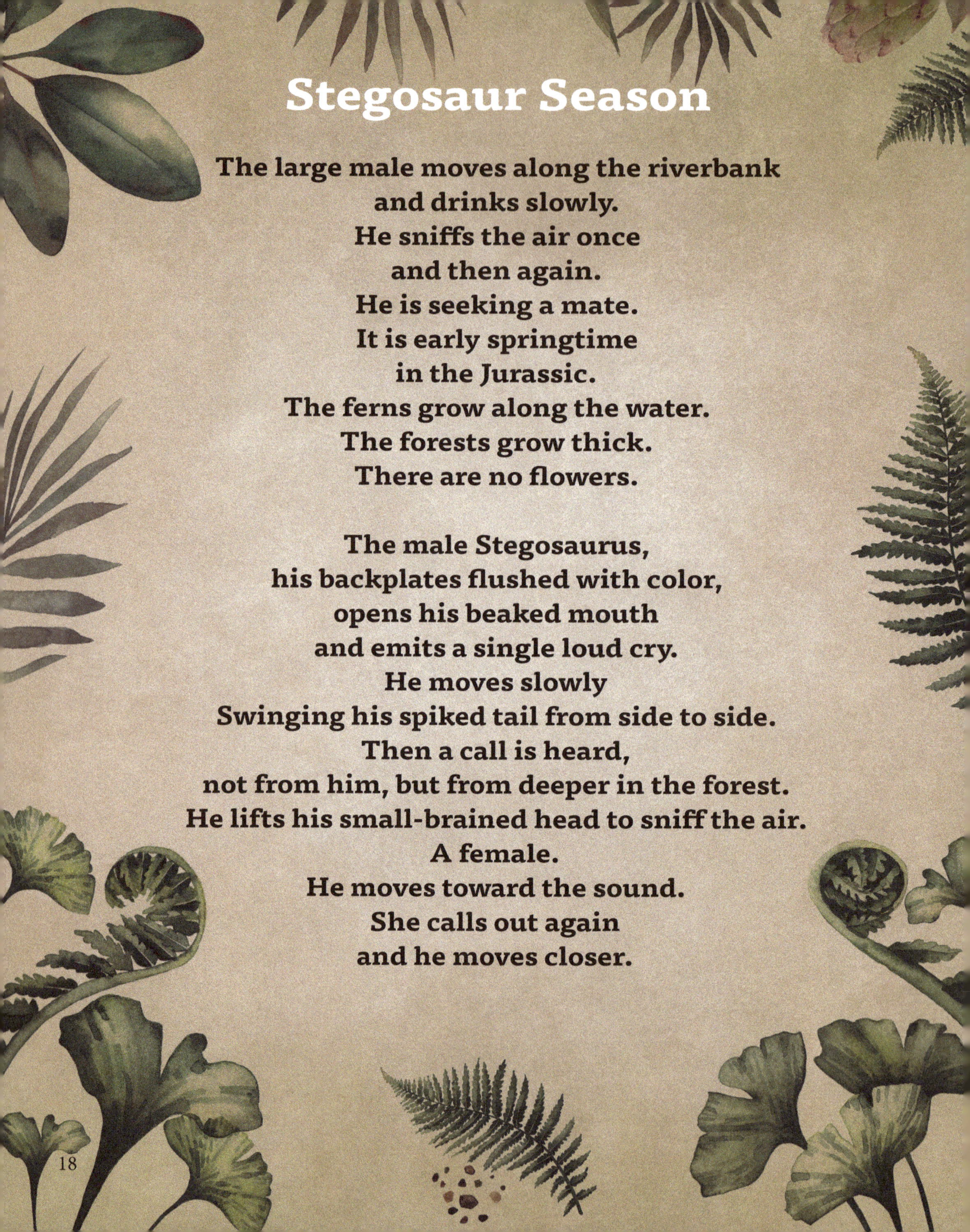

Stegosaur Season

The large male moves along the riverbank
and drinks slowly.
He sniffs the air once
and then again.
He is seeking a mate.
It is early springtime
in the Jurassic.
The ferns grow along the water.
The forests grow thick.
There are no flowers.

The male Stegosaurus,
his backplates flushed with color,
opens his beaked mouth
and emits a single loud cry.
He moves slowly
Swinging his spiked tail from side to side.
Then a call is heard,
not from him, but from deeper in the forest.
He lifts his small-brained head to sniff the air.
A female.
He moves toward the sound.
She calls out again
and he moves closer.

He is almost upon her
when his small eyes see her.
They circle around each other cautiously.
Their babies will hatch
later in the spring.

Time of the Hunt

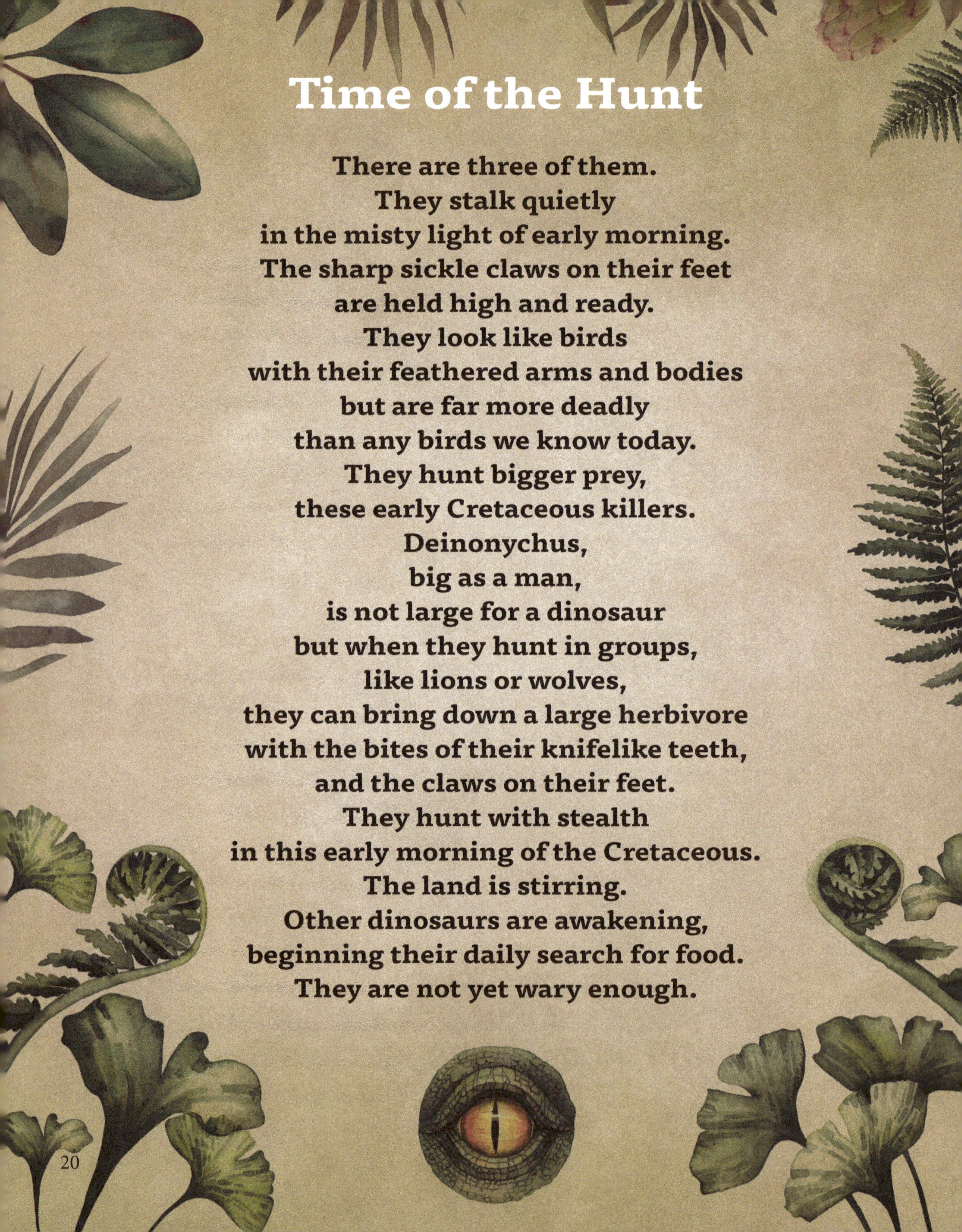

There are three of them.
They stalk quietly
in the misty light of early morning.
The sharp sickle claws on their feet
are held high and ready.
They look like birds
with their feathered arms and bodies
but are far more deadly
than any birds we know today.
They hunt bigger prey,
these early Cretaceous killers.
Deinonychus,
big as a man,
is not large for a dinosaur
but when they hunt in groups,
like lions or wolves,
they can bring down a large herbivore
with the bites of their knifelike teeth,
and the claws on their feet.
They hunt with stealth
in this early morning of the Cretaceous.
The land is stirring.
Other dinosaurs are awakening,
beginning their daily search for food.
They are not yet wary enough.

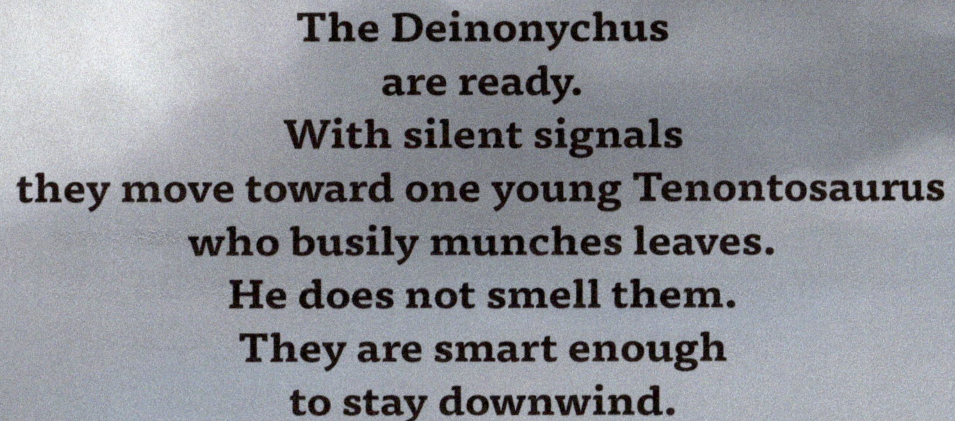

The Deinonychus
are ready.
With silent signals
they move toward one young Tenontosaurus
who busily munches leaves.
He does not smell them.
They are smart enough
to stay downwind.

Suddenly
one Deinonychus jumps,
a great leap,
which lands her on the back of the plant-eater.
He groans and tries to shake her off
but her companions leap as well.
With teeth and sickle claws ready
they bring down their large prey.
They will rest that afternoon
well fed.

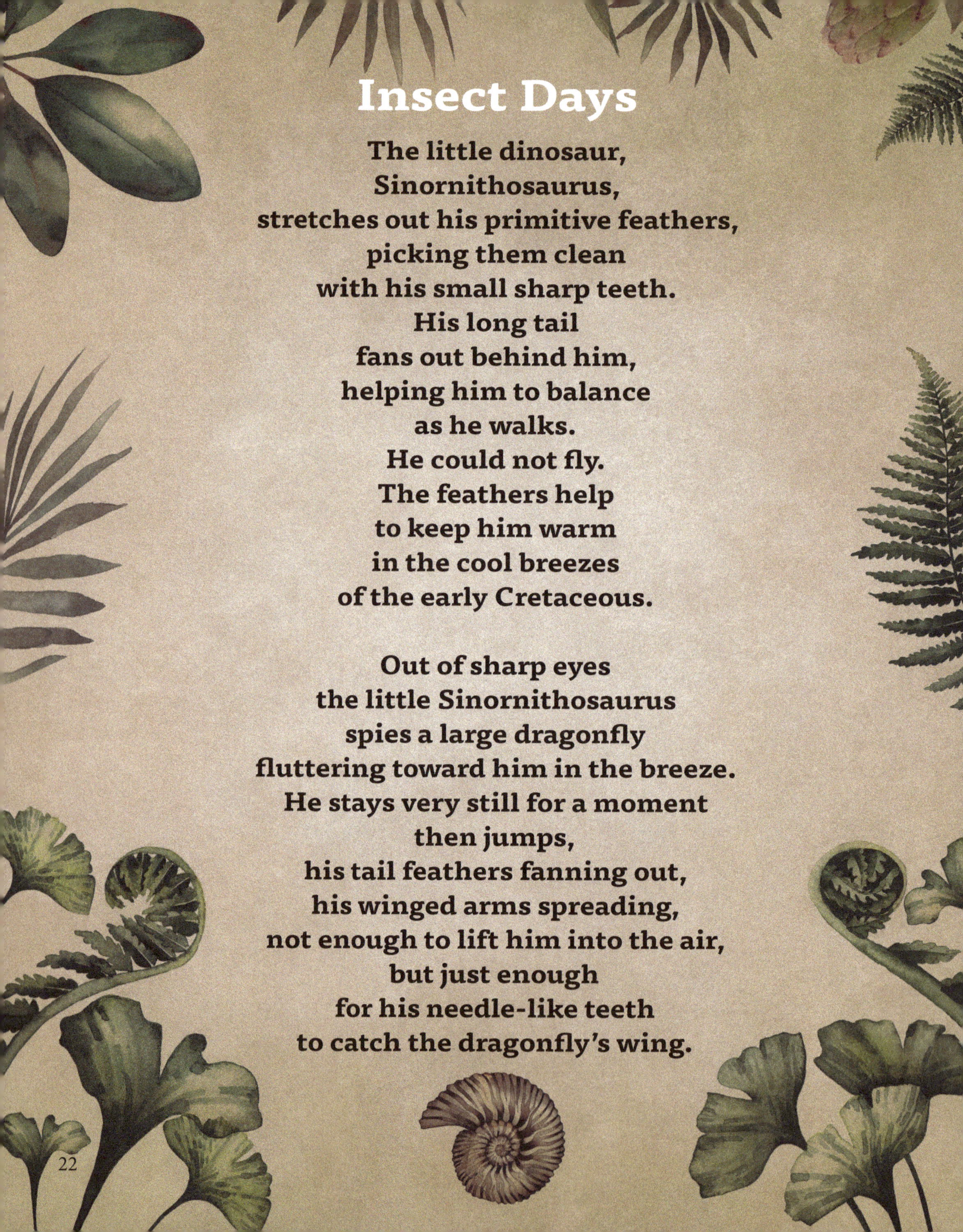

Insect Days

The little dinosaur,
Sinornithosaurus,
stretches out his primitive feathers,
picking them clean
with his small sharp teeth.
His long tail
fans out behind him,
helping him to balance
as he walks.
He could not fly.
The feathers help
to keep him warm
in the cool breezes
of the early Cretaceous.

Out of sharp eyes
the little Sinornithosaurus
spies a large dragonfly
fluttering toward him in the breeze.
He stays very still for a moment
then jumps,
his tail feathers fanning out,
his winged arms spreading,
not enough to lift him into the air,
but just enough
for his needle-like teeth
to catch the dragonfly's wing.

As the Sinornithosaurus
crunches his insect dinner,
the dragonfly's second wing
breaks off, fluttering in rainbow colors
to the ground.

Hatching Season

A large circle
of ferns and greens
lay on the ground.
Nearby
other circles of green.
They had lain there for a season
weathering the wind and rain and sun.
Now it was time.

A faint sound of tapping,
then another,
then a hundred tapping sounds
fill the air.
The mother Maiasaurs,
drowsing,
raise their heads to listen.
Then
another sound,
the sound of eggshells cracking,
as the little Maiasaurs
push their way out
into the world.

The newborn dinosaurs
make small peeping sounds
as they walk on wobbly legs
around the nests,
waiting for their mothers
to bring them their first meal.
They were tiny now
but they would grow
very fast.
They had to grow fast
in this rough world
full of large-toothed predators.
But for now,

for just a little while,
they would be safe.
For now,
for just a little while,
their mothers would take care of
them.

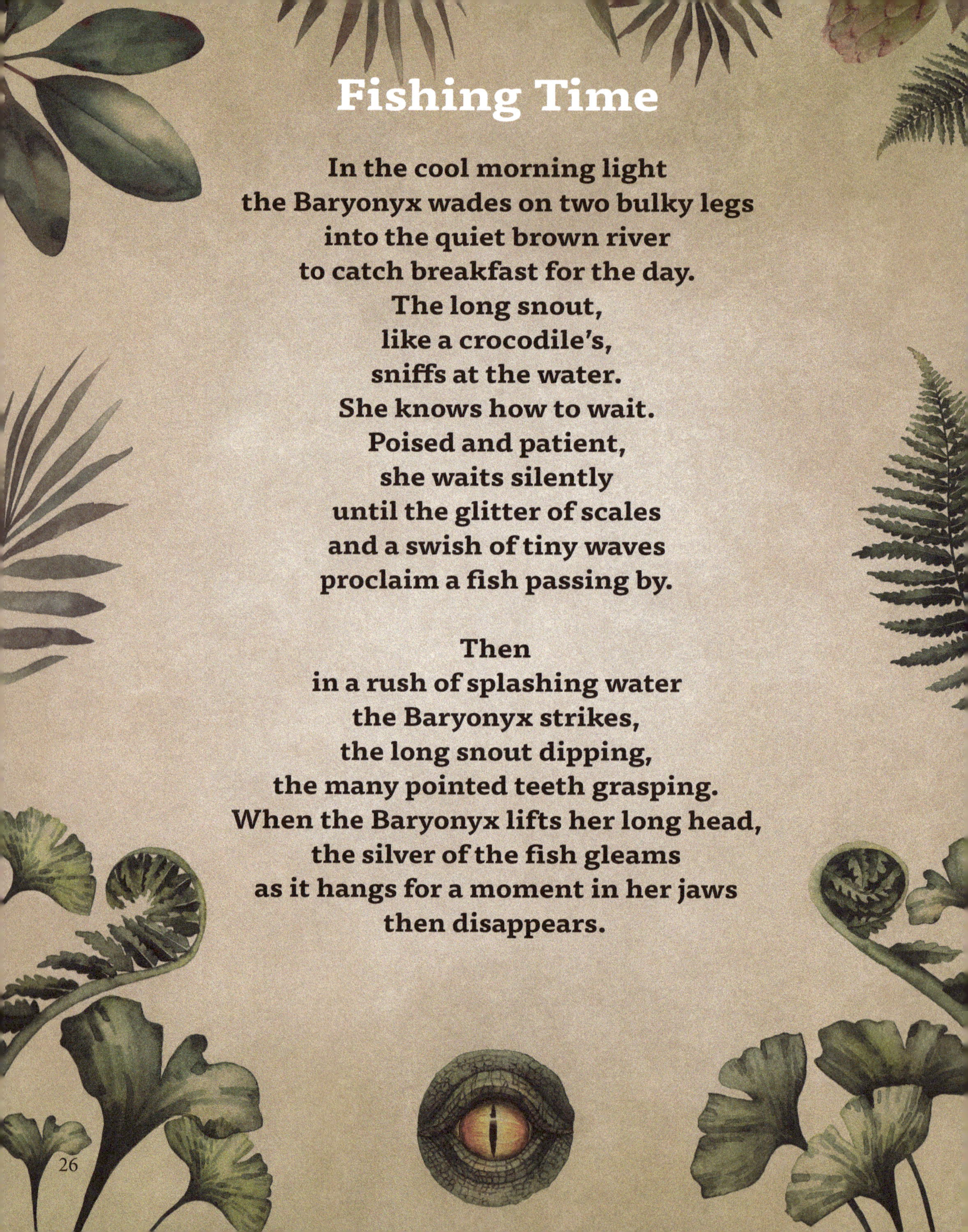

Fishing Time

In the cool morning light
the Baryonyx wades on two bulky legs
into the quiet brown river
to catch breakfast for the day.
The long snout,
like a crocodile's,
sniffs at the water.
She knows how to wait.
Poised and patient,
she waits silently
until the glitter of scales
and a swish of tiny waves
proclaim a fish passing by.

Then
in a rush of splashing water
the Baryonyx strikes,
the long snout dipping,
the many pointed teeth grasping.
When the Baryonyx lifts her long head,
the silver of the fish gleams
as it hangs for a moment in her jaws
then disappears.

Therizinosaur Afternoon

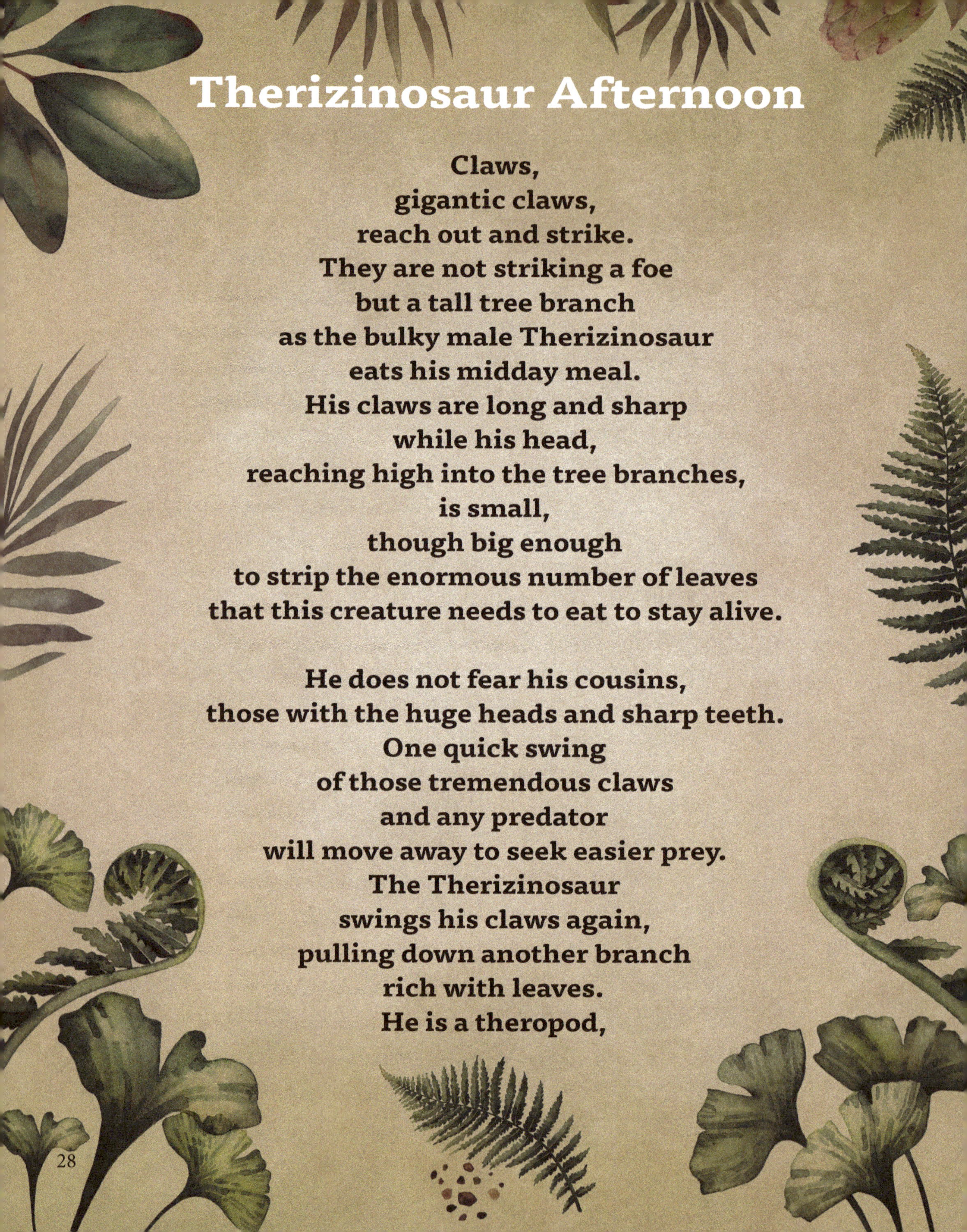

Claws,
gigantic claws,
reach out and strike.
They are not striking a foe
but a tall tree branch
as the bulky male Therizinosaur
eats his midday meal.
His claws are long and sharp
while his head,
reaching high into the tree branches,
is small,
though big enough
to strip the enormous number of leaves
that this creature needs to eat to stay alive.

He does not fear his cousins,
those with the huge heads and sharp teeth.
One quick swing
of those tremendous claws
and any predator
will move away to seek easier prey.
The Therizinosaur
swings his claws again,
pulling down another branch
rich with leaves.
He is a theropod,

evolved from the meat-eaters of the Mesozoic
but he has evolved into
an herbivorous theropod,
a weird creature living
in the twilight of Dinosaur Time.

Pterosaur Morning

Dawn breaks pink
in the Eastern sky
shining on Quetzalcoatlus,
one of the largest flying creatures
the Earth has ever seen.

As big as a small airplane when in flight,
as tall as a giraffe when on the ground,
the Quetzalcoatlus
stretches his wings in the morning light
picking tiny insects off
with his long odd-shaped beak,
careful not to bite through his own skin.
The Quetzalcoatlus
walks across the sandy beach,
a gawky and strange figure with no grace,
tilting this way and that.
He moves awkwardly but surely,
using the hands on his wings
for balance.

Then
sensing the rising currents of air,
he stretches his wings out
to take to the sky.
Suddenly
he is a figure of beauty and grace,
his enormous head stretched out,
his head dipping
as he searches the water for food.
A soft fine fuzz of proto feathers
covers his body.
He basks
on the waves of air
warmed by the late Cretaceous sun.

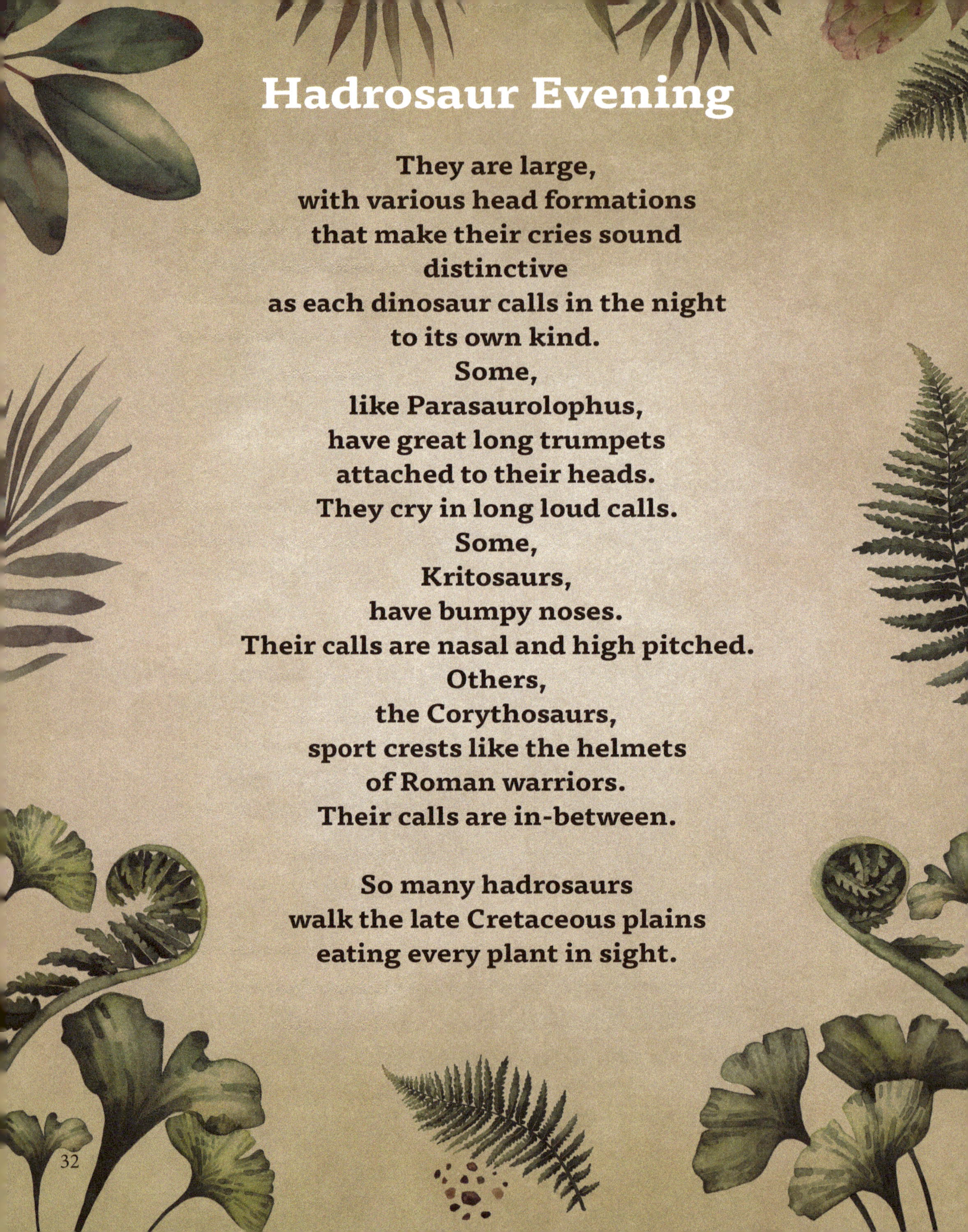

Hadrosaur Evening

They are large,
with various head formations
that make their cries sound
distinctive
as each dinosaur calls in the night
to its own kind.
Some,
like Parasaurolophus,
have great long trumpets
attached to their heads.
They cry in long loud calls.
Some,
Kritosaurs,
have bumpy noses.
Their calls are nasal and high pitched.
Others,
the Corythosaurs,
sport crests like the helmets
of Roman warriors.
Their calls are in-between.

So many hadrosaurs
walk the late Cretaceous plains
eating every plant in sight.

At night they slow,
rest,
call to each other.
The Cretaceous evening
echoes with their cries
and the heat of the evening
as it turns into night
carries their calls for miles.

Triceratops Twilight

A call,
a mother to her young.
The young
rolls on the ground,
reveling in play, the task of the young
of all species, all times.
He does not yet know
what the mother has learned from experience;
that the Cretaceous world is full of danger
and that sometimes with evening
the great hunters hunt.
They have their keen sense of smell
to guide them in the dimming light.

The mother calls
and the young Triceratops goes to her.
Some Triceratops, being herbivores,
live in herds that roam the low plains,
grazing on the newborn leaves and flowering plants
that have evolved in the evening of the Mesozoic.
These dinosaurs do not know
that they are the last of their kind.
They only know
that they must avoid the great predators
to live another day.
All the mothers
and all the young
gather around in the gloom of twilight,
the adults on the edges,
the young in the center.
They close their eyes
to rest as night falls.

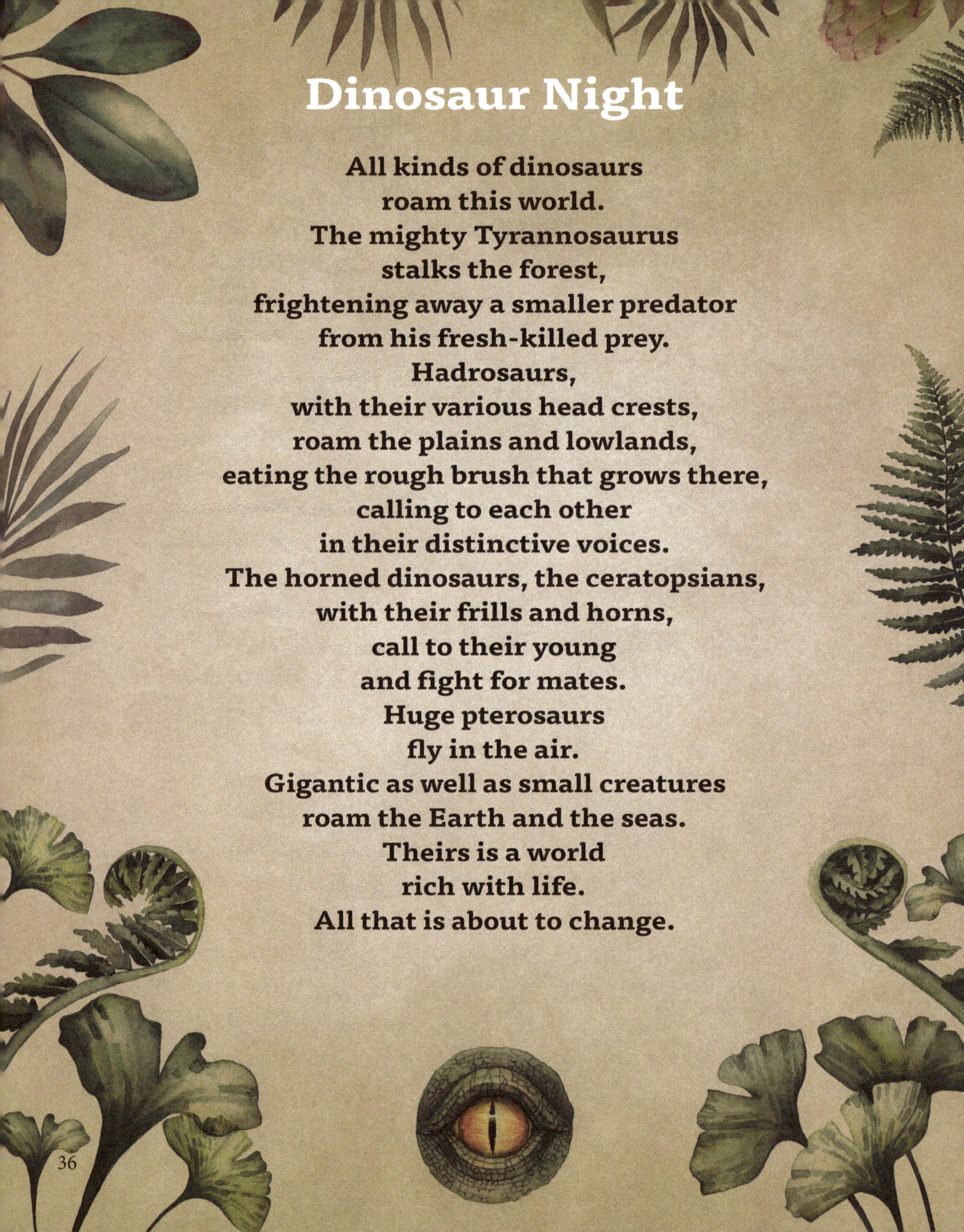

Dinosaur Night

All kinds of dinosaurs
roam this world.
The mighty Tyrannosaurus
stalks the forest,
frightening away a smaller predator
from his fresh-killed prey.
Hadrosaurs,
with their various head crests,
roam the plains and lowlands,
eating the rough brush that grows there,
calling to each other
in their distinctive voices.
The horned dinosaurs, the ceratopsians,
with their frills and horns,
call to their young
and fight for mates.
Huge pterosaurs
fly in the air.
Gigantic as well as small creatures
roam the Earth and the seas.
Theirs is a world
rich with life.
All that is about to change.

At first
it is just a roar of wind.
All of the Earth's creatures
continue to feed, to play, to rest.
But then comes
a rush of noise so loud and terrible
it has never before been heard on Earth.
The ground shakes.
Nothing is as it was before.

The asteroid has struck.

A wave of darkness
begins to move over the world,
a terrible darkness
that brings fire and ice
in its wake.
There is no clean air to breathe,
no green plants.
The oceans suffocate.
The Earth goes into a long sleep.

When it awakens
there are no more dinosaurs
except…
up in the sky
a winged creature flies.
Her wings are blue and gold.
Her head stretches toward the newborn sun.
There are no more dinosaurs
like those who had come before
but the birds,
avian dinosaurs,
fill the skies,
swim the waters,
build their nests.

Life
continues on.
And in some manner
those ancient dinosaurs are still here.
In the dry soil of the mesa
a human
sees a bit of white,
knows it is a bone.
It is the bone of a dinosaur
exposed by wind and weather
in this rough cliff face.
The bones of the ancient ones
remain in the Earth
for us to find,
to re-create a world long lost;
to find what is left of those mighty dinosaurs,
those large and small, quick and fierce,
those of feathers and those of teeth and horns,
and bring them back to life again.

Afterword

Paleontologists know more than ever about dinosaurs, and we are learning more every day. We currently live in the golden age of dinosaur discovery. But while scientists know more than ever about dinosaurs, there is much we do not know. We can conjecture what the lives of various species looked like, but we do not know for sure.

In this, the second edition of Dinosaur Seasons, I have made some modifications from the first book based on recent discoveries. I have also taken some artistic license to build portraits of the living animals and their lifestyles. For example, most fossils of Triceratops have been found alone, while those of other ceratopsians have sometimes been found in groups. However, a recent discovery found three juvenile Triceratops buried together. Is it that far off from probability to conjecture that the young may have lived with adults for a time, as I have described them in this book?

There is so much we have yet to learn. Perhaps future editions of this book or a new book altogether, will incorporate the new discoveries being made of the ever-fascinating creatures we call dinosaurs.

Resources

Courses:

- *Geology 104, Dinosaurs: A Natural History posted on* YouTube by Dr. Thomas Holtz, University of Maryland
- Coursera has free courses on dinosaurs from the University of Alberta; *Dino 101* and *Theropod Dinosaurs and the Origin of Birds.*

Books for Adults:

- *Dinosaurs Rediscovered by* Michael J. Benton
- *Dinosaur Odyssey by* Scott D. Samson
- *The Rise and Fall of the Dinosaurs by* Steve Brusatte

Books for Children:

- *National Geographic Little Kids First Big Book of Dinosaurs by* Catherine D. Hughes and Franco Tempesta
- *The Magnificent Book of Dinosaurs and Other Prehistoric Creatures by* Tom Jackson and Rudolf Farcas
- *Inside Dinosaurs by* Andra Serlin Abramson and Carl Mehling

Podcasts:

- *I Know Dino*-a podcast full of information on new dinosaur discoveries

Museums:

- Natural history museums- wonderful places where you can learn more about these wonderful and amazing creatures

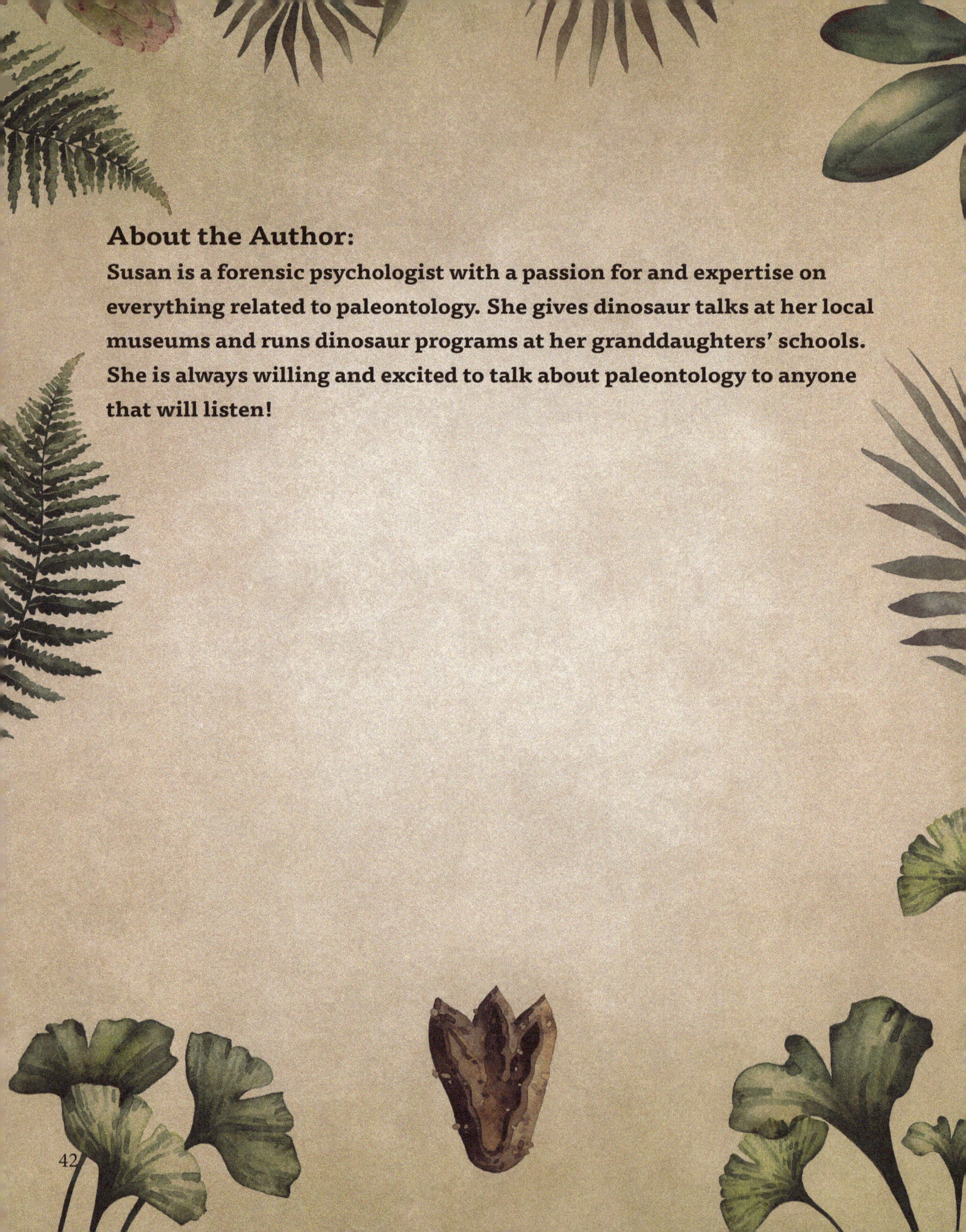

About the Author:

Susan is a forensic psychologist with a passion for and expertise on everything related to paleontology. She gives dinosaur talks at her local museums and runs dinosaur programs at her granddaughters' schools. She is always willing and excited to talk about paleontology to anyone that will listen!